Wild Women
TALK ABOUT Love

Varla Ventura

Conari Press

First published in 2007 by Conari Press,
an imprint of Red Wheel/Weiser, LLC
With offices at:
500 Third Street, Suite 230
San Francisco, CA 94107
www.redwheelweiser.com

ISBN 10:1-57324-291-8
ISBN 13:978-1-57324-291-2

Library of Congress Cataloging-in-Publication Data available upon request

Cover and book design by Suzanne Albertson
Typeset in Wilke
Cover photograph © Wright Card and Gift

Printed in Canada
TCP
10 9 8 7 6 5 4 3 2 1

CONTENTS

INTRODUCTION

One hour of right-down love is worth an age of dully living on.
—*Aphra Behn, creator of the seventeenth-century forerunner of the modern novel*

I f there's one thing that's been on the minds of all wild women for as long as we've been around, it's love. And since wild women have been on the scene right from the very beginning, it's safe to say that we've accumulated a veritable stockpile of wit and wisdom on the subject of amour—both good and bad. Whether the topic at hand is true love, lost love, scandalous love, or even (heaven forbid) unrequited love, we've always got a good story or inspiring motto to share.

That's the idea behind this latest addition to the Wild Women library. What better way to celebrate our past, present, and future than with a book devoted to one of our favorite subjects? There are as many kinds of wild love out there as there are wild women, and that's certainly something worth honoring. With this in mind, there's much more to this book than your usual Valentine's card sentiment (although there's plenty of that for you true romantics to enjoy). In the chapters that follow, you'll find reflections on everything from the joys of new love to the heartbreak of divorce, from lust and sex to loving someone of the same sex. It's all part of what makes us so wonderfully wild, and it's all part of this book as well.

So whether you're in the middle of a lasting romance, starting something new, or even recovering from your last tangle with Cupid's arrows, there's a quote here that will speak to you. And with legends and life stories of some of the most famous amorous women included in each chapter, you'll be inspired as well as entertained. Love has always been a part of our lives; keep embracing its wildness and add your own stories to those that have come before!

Love Is Fabulous

Love at first sight is easy to understand; it's when two people have been looking at each other for a lifetime that it becomes a miracle.

—*Amy Bloom, story-writing shrink*

There is no substitute for the comfort supplied by the utterly taken-for-granted relationship.

—*Iris Murdoch, British author*

The only abnormality is the incapacity to love.

—*Anaïs Nin, passionate writer*

Anyone can be passionate, but it takes real lovers to be silly.

—*Rose Franken, manuscript maker*

I'm not good at being alone. Especially at the end of the day when my finances are a mess, my car is falling apart, [and] I can't find my shoes. That's when I need a big strong guy to hold me close so I can look deep into his eyes and blame him.

—*Simone Alexander, stand-up girl*

Love is the difficult realization that something other than oneself is real.

—*Iris Murdoch, British author*

I have no patience with women who measure and weigh their love like a country doctor dispensing capsules. If a man is worth loving at all, he is worth loving generously, even recklessly.

—*Marie Dressler, character actress of the thirties*

You'll discover that real love is millions of miles past falling in love with anyone or anything. When you make that one effort to feel compassion instead of blame or self-blame, the heart opens again and continues opening.

—*Sara Paddison, self-help guru*

Our true identity is to love without fear and insecurity. Our higher potential finds us when we set our course in that direction. The power of love and compassion transforms insecurity.

—*Doc Childre, physician of motivation*

Divine Love always has met and always will meet every human need.

—*Mary Baker Eddy, spiritual leader*

The greatest science in the world, in heaven and on earth, is love.

—*Mother Teresa, legendary selfless philanthropist*

Never let a problem to be solved become more important than a person to be loved.

—*Barbara Johnson, feminist and professor*

Love doesn't just sit there, like a stone; it has to be made, like bread, remade all the time, made new.

—*Ursula K. LeGuin, imaginative author and poet*

I have never met a person whose greatest need was anything other than real, unconditional love. . . . There is no mistaking love. You feel it in your heart. It is the common fiber of life, the flame that heats our soul, energizes our spirit and supplies passion to our lives.

—*Elizabeth Kubler-Ross, psychiatrist and love expert*

If I am unaware of love, I live drably. If I become intoxicated with love, I live in dreamland. If I recognize love and shake his hand, then comfort, dreams, and sometimes intoxication become mine to drench in and give away as well.

—*Nellie Curtiss, passionate author*

Where there is great love there are always miracles.

—*Willa Cather, Pulitzer Prize-winning author*

Loves conquers all things except poverty and toothache.

—*Mae West, legend of the silver screen*

Love is like pi—natural, irrational, and VERY important.

—*Lisa Hoffman, intellectual and humorous writer*

Oshun

Known in Africa as the Mother of the River, Oshun is the Yoruba goddess of love, sensuality, and beauty. Though she is said to have a fierce temper when crossed, she most often uses her powers for the benefit of mankind. During the creation of the world, the blacksmith Ogun became tired of working and abandoned his tasks, retreating into the forest. Oshun entered the woods to draw him out, dancing and beguiling him with her splendor. Ogun was so inspired by her loveliness that he took up his tools with more skill and power than he had ever shown before.

Oshun is also a deity of courage and determination. In ancient times, humankind rebelled against Olodumare, the Lord of Heaven, and refused to serve him. Enraged, Olodumare brought a drought upon the earth, and the people were afflicted with famine. Birds were sent to beg for the Lord's forgiveness, but none of them was able to fly high enough to reach his house in the sun. Oshun, in the form of a peacock, was the only one to complete the journey; by the time she arrived, her beautiful feathers had been burned black as a vulture's. Moved by her bravery, Olodumare restored her and ended the drought, naming her an honored Messenger of his house. As the embodiment of love, Oshun combines sexual allure and beauty with a strength that can overcome all obstacles.

Love and magic have a great deal in common. They enrich the soul, delight the heart. And they both take practice.

—*Nora Roberts, first author inducted into the*
Romance Writers of America Hall of Fame

Love is the best medicine, and there is more than enough to go around once you open your heart.

—Julie Marie, thoughtful wild woman

He has achieved success who has lived well, laughed often, and loved much.

—Bessie Stanley, wise and modest poet

To fall in love is easy, even to remain in it is not difficult; our human loneliness is cause enough. But it is a hard quest worth making to find a comrade through whose steady presence one becomes steadily the person one desires to be.

—*Anna Louise Strong, progressive journalist*

Whatever our souls are made of, his and mine are the same.

—*Emily Brontë, famed romantic novelist*

Love is a force more formidable than any other. It is invisible—it cannot be seen or measured, yet it is powerful enough to transform you in a moment, and offer you more joy than any material possession could.

—*Barbara De Angelis, motivational author and speaker*

Infatuation is when you think he's as sexy as Robert Redford, as smart as Henry Kissinger, as noble as Ralph Nader, as funny as Woody Allen, and as athletic as Jimmy Conners. Love is when you realize that he's as sexy as Woody Allen, as smart as Jimmy Connors, as funny as Ralph Nader, as athletic as Henry Kissinger and nothing like Robert Redford—but you'll take him anyway.

—*Judith Viorst, author of children's books*

Hate leaves ugly scars, love leaves beautiful ones.

—Mignon McLaughlin, journalist and author

Love never reasons but profusely gives; gives, like a thoughtless prodigal, its all, and trembles lest it has done too little.

—Hannah Moore, romantic author

Love makes your soul crawl out from its hiding place.

—Zora Neale Hurston, barrier-breaking novelist

Love is a game that two can play and both win.

—Eva Gabor, Hungarian-born diva

There's nothing more freeing than the shackles of love.

—*Emma Racine deFleur, free-spirited writer*

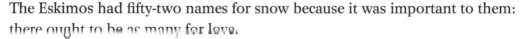

The Eskimos had fifty-two names for snow because it was important to them: there ought to be as many for love.

—*Margaret Atwood, famed feminist author*

Nobody has ever measured, even poets, how much a heart can hold.

—Zelda Fitzgerald, author and quintessential twenties flapper

Love, like a river, will cut a new path whenever it meets an obstacle.

—Crystal Middlemas, passionate wild woman

When you love someone, all your saved-up wishes start coming out.

—Elizabeth Bowen, Anglo-Irish author

Love is smiling on the inside and out.

—Jennifer Williams, amorous optimist

The truth [is] that there is only one terminal dignity—love. And the story of a love is not important—what is important is that one is capable of love. It is perhaps the only glimpse we are permitted of eternity.

—Helen Hayes, nicknamed "First Lady of the American Theater"

Love is a moment that lasts forever. . . .

—*Julie Wittey, romantic writing woman*

The best and most beautiful things in this world cannot be seen or even heard, but must be felt with the heart.

—*Helen Keller, legendary deaf-blind activist*

Love reminds you that nothing else matters.

—*Amy Bushell, prioritizing wild woman*

The dedicated life is the life worth living. You must give with your
whole heart

—*Annie Dillard, philosophical American author*

Some people come into our lives and quickly go. Some people move our souls to dance. They awaken us to new understanding with the passing whisper of their wisdom. Some people make the sky more beautiful to gaze upon. They stay in our lives for awhile, leave footprints on our hearts, and we are never ever the same.

—Flavia Weedn, crafter of inspirational art and writing

Romance is the glamour which turns the dust of everyday life into a golden haze.

—Elynor Glyn, inspired author

Love is not a matter of counting the years . . . but of making the years count.

—*Michelle St. Amand, writer and loving wild woman*

I have learned not to worry about love; But to honor its coming with all my heart.

—*Alice Walker, award-winning African American author*

I love you—those three words have my life in them.

—Alexandra Romanov, the last czarina, to husband Nicholas II

We can only learn to love by loving.

—Iris Murdoch, British author

Love is the mortar that holds the human structure together.

—Karen Casey, advice-giving author

I am like a falling star who has finally found her place next to another in a lovely constellation, where we will sparkle in the heavens forever.

—*Amy Tan, Chinese American novelist*

If you have love in your life it can make up for a great many things you lack. If you don't have it, no matter what else there is, it's not enough.

—*Ann Landers, advice column queen bee*

Love is a choice you make from moment to moment.

—*Barbara De Angelis, motivational author and speaker*

Who so loves, believes the impossible.

—*Elizabeth Barrett Browning, British Victorian poet*

Love is more than a feeling; it's a state of mind.

—Lisa Grude, perceptive wild woman

That Love is all there is,
Is all we know of Love.

—Emily Dickinson, legendary and mysterious American poet

Love and Marriage

We've all heard the saying; whether we like it or not, the two do seem to go together. From rhapsodizing about the lasting joys to bitching about the equally consistent irritations, women have the corner on marriage talk. The sampling below is nowhere near everything we could have said!

The married are those who have taken the terrible risk of intimacy and, having taken it, know life without intimacy to be impossible.

—*Carolyn Heilbrun, feminist and academic author*

I love being married. It's so great to find that one special person you want to annoy for the rest of your life.

—*Rita Rudner, sovereign of stand-up*

I married the first man I ever kissed. When I tell my children that they just about throw up.

—Barbara Bush, devoted First Lady

I've had an exciting time. I married for love and got a little money along with it.

—Rose Fitzgerald Kennedy, matriarch of the Kennedy clan

Marriage is a matter of give and take, but so far I haven't been able to find anybody who'll take what I have to give.

—Cass Daley, bold actress

Marrying a man is like buying something you've been admiring for a long time in a shop window. You may love it when you get it home, but it doesn't always go with everything else in the house.

—Jean Kerr, humorous author and playwright

I must quit marrying men who feel inferior to me. Somewhere there must be a man who could be my husband and not feel inferior. I need a superior inferior man.

—*Hedy Lamarr, Tinseltown luminary*

The trouble with some women is they get all excited about nothing—and then they marry him.

—*Cher, persevering pop icon*

If the husband and wife can possibly afford it, they should definitely have separate bathrooms for the sake of the marriage.

—*Doris Day, perky film legend*

My husband and I celebrated our thirty-eighth wedding anniversary. You know what I realized? If I had killed the man the first time I thought about it, I'd have been out of jail by now.

—*Anita Miller, candid comedian*

I had to really cut down on my dating.

>—*Sarah Michelle Gellar, actress, on how marriage changed her life*

Before accepting a marriage proposal, take a good look at his father. If he's still handsome, witty, and has all his teeth ... marry him instead.

>—*Diane Jordan, humorist*

An archaeologist is the best husband a woman can have. The older she gets the more interested he is in her.

>—*Agatha Christie, literary woman of mystery*

One advantage of marriage, it seems to me, is that when you fall out of love with him or he falls out of love with you, it keeps you together until maybe you fall in again.

>—*Judith Viorst, author of children's books*

Age does not protect you from love, but love to some extent protects you from age.

—*Jeanne Moreau, French leading lady*

Love vanquishes time. To lovers, a moment can be eternity, eternity can be the tick of a clock.

—*Mary Parrish, sage and author*

I truly feel that there are as many ways of loving as there are people in the world and as there are days in the life of those people.

—*Mary S. Calderone, pioneering physician of sexuality*

But one of the attributes of love, like art, is to bring harmony and order out of chaos, to introduce meaning and affect where before there was none, to give rhythmic variations, highs and lows to a landscape that was previously flat.

—*Molly Haskell, author and theatre critic*

Who has not found the heaven below
Will fail of it above.
God's residence is next to mine,
His furniture is love.

—*Emily Dickinson, legendary and mysterious American poet*

What the world really needs is more love and less paperwork.

—*Pearl Bailey, respected African American actress*

The person who tries to live alone will not succeed as a human being. His heart withers if it does not answer another heart. His mind shrinks away if he hears only the echoes of his own thoughts and finds no other inspiration.

—*Pearl S. Buck, Nobel Prize-winning author*

Do you want me to tell you something really subversive? Love is everything it's cracked up to be. That's why people are so cynical about it. It really is worth fighting for, being brave for, risking everything for. And the trouble is, if you don't risk anything, you risk even more.

—*Erica Jong, American author of women's lit*

A man has only one escape from his old self: to see a different self in the mirror of some woman's eyes.

—Clare Boothe Luce, author and bold activist

If there is any country on earth where the course of true love may be expected to run smooth, it is America.

—Harriet Martineau, British writer of the 1800s

Art is not necessary at all. All that is necessary to make this world a better place to live in is to love—to love as Christ loved, as Buddha loved.

—Isadora Duncan, queen of modern dance

I don't want to live—I want to love first, and live incidentally

—Zelda Fitzgerald, author and quintessential twenties flapper

Love is a great beautifier.

—*Louisa May Alcott, great nineteenth-century women's novelist*

Love's greatest gift is its ability to make everything it touches sacred.

—*Barbara De Angelis, motivational author and speaker*

Not all of us have to possess earthshaking talent. Just common sense and love will do.

—*Myrtle Auvil, wild artist and author*

Love alone could waken love.

—*Pearl S. Buck, Nobel Prize-winning author*

Melissa Gregory

When ice dancer Melissa Gregory found herself searching for a skating partner in early 2000, she didn't realize that she was about to encounter her life partner as well. Gregory had been building a successful track record in the sport, winning first place in the junior level at the U.S. Nationals. But when her partner decided to return to school, she turned to the Internet to help find his replacement. That was where fate, and Denis Petukhov, stepped in. After corresponding by e-mail, the two decided to meet in person and explore the possibility of a working partnership.

Petukhov flew to the United States for the tryout, and he and Gregory spent a morning skating together. Upon getting off the ice, Petukhov canceled his other scheduled tryouts; he never used his return ticket to Russia and has kept it to this day. The pair soon realized that their connection went well beyond the sport, and they were married in 2001. Since then, they have risen through the ice dancing ranks, earning several international medals. Petukhov became a U.S. citizen in February 2005, allowing them to try for a spot on the 2006 Olympic team. Although the couple has faced hurdles ranging from dangerous falls to a hostile reception in Petukhov's native Russia, the future looks bright for Gregory and her partner both on and off the ice.

If it is your time, love will track you down like a cruise missile.
—*Lynda Barry, progressive cartoonist*

Real love is a pilgrimage. It happens when there is no strategy, but it is very rare because most people are strategists.

—*Anita Brookner, English art historian and writer*

Love comes when manipulation stops; when you think more about the other person than about his or her reactions to you. When you dare to reveal yourself fully. When you dare to be vulnerable.

—*Joyce Brothers, columnist and family psychologist*

To love without role, without power plays, is revolution.

—*Rita Mae Brown, activist author*

How do I love thee? Let me count the ways.
I love thee to the depth and breadth and height
my soul can reach. . .

—*Elizabeth Barrett Browning, famed Victorian poet*

You can give without loving, but you cannot love without giving.

—*Amy Carmichael, inspirational British missionary*

The cure for all the ills and wrongs, the cares, the sorrows, and the crimes of humanity, all lie in that one word "Love." It is the divine vitality that everywhere produces and restores life.

—*Lydia M. Child, American abolitionist and writer*

Every day I live I am more convinced that the waste of life lies in the love we have not given, the powers we have not used, the selfish prudence that will risk nothing and which, shirking pain, misses happiness as well.

—*Mary Cholmondeley, independent British author*

Love makes the wildest spirit tame, and the tamest spirit wild.

—*Alexis Delp, author and true wild woman*

I know that I can give love for a minute, for half an hour, for a day, for a month, but I can give, and I'm very happy to do that and I want to do that.

—*Diana, Princess of Wales*

I argue thee that love is life. And life hath immortality.

—*Emily Dickinson, legendary and mysterious American poet*

We've grown to be one soul—two parts; our lives so intertwined that when some passion stirs your heart, I feel the quake in mine.

—Gloria Gaither, inspired gospel musician

Love has nothing to do with what you are expecting to get, only what you are expecting to give—which is everything.

—Katharine Hepburn, bold and beautiful screen legend

Love is a force that connects us to every strand of the universe, an unconditional state that characterizes human nature, a form of knowledgement that is always there for us if only we can open ourselves to it.

—Emily H. Sell, editor and author

Falling in love consists merely in uncorking the imagination and bottling the common sense.

—Helen Rowland, witty journalist

To infinite, ever present Love, all is Love, and there is no error, no sin, sickness, nor death.

—*Mary Baker Eddy, spiritual leader*

Put love first. Entertain thoughts that give life. And when a thought or resentment, or hurt, or fear comes your way, have another thought that is more powerful—a thought that is love.

—*Mary Manin Morrissey, inspirational minister*

You never lose by loving. You always lose by holding back.

—*Barbara DeAngelis, motivational author and speaker*

Sleeping alone, except under doctor's orders, does much harm. Children will tell you how lonely it is sleeping alone. If possible, you should always sleep with someone you love. You both recharge your mutual batteries free of charge.

—*Marlene Dietrich, film legend*

Love is a gift of one's innermost soul to another so both can be whole.

—*Tea Rose, generous wild woman*

There isn't any formula or method. You learn to love by loving— by paying attention and doing what one thereby discovers has to be done.

—*Helen Hayes, nicknamed the "First Lady of American Theatre"*

To love is to receive a glimpse of heaven.

—*Karen Sunde, playwright and screenwriter*

There is always something left to love. And if you haven't learned that, you ain't learned nothing.

—*Lorraine Hansberry, famed and respected playwright*

Love involves a peculiar unfathomable combination of understanding and misunderstanding.

—*Diane Arbus, wild female photographer*

It is better to break one's heart than to do nothing with it.

—*Margaret Kennedy, risk-taking lady*

Love is always present, it is just a matter of feeling it or not.

—Kimberly Kirberg, loving wild woman

To love means not to impose your own powers on your fellow man but offer him your help. And if he refuses it, to be proud that he can do it on his own strength.

—Elizabeth Kubler-Ross, psychiatrist and love expert

Love is the emblem of eternity; it confounds all notions of time; effaces all memory of beginning, all fear of an end.

—*Madame de Stael, literary figure of old Paris*

Life is infested with ordinariness and there is no reason why love should be, too.

—*Daphne Rose Kingma, who literally wrote* The Book of Love

The more connections you and your lover make, not just between your bodies, but between your minds, your hearts, and your souls, the more you will strengthen the fabric of your relationship, and the more real moments you will experience together.

—*Barbara De Angelis, motivational author and speaker*

One kind word can warm three winter months.

—*Mary Jane Ryan, happiness-spreading author*

To love deeply in one direction makes us more loving in all others.

—*Madame Anne Swetchine, intellectual and mystic*

Love means never having to say "What?"

—*Autumn Stephens, the original wild woman herself*

What did my hands do before they held you?

—*Sylvia Plath, passionate and tragic poet*

CHAPTER 2

Lustful Love

Lovers are like roses—best by the dozen.

—*Barbara La Marr, silent film starlet*

You know more about a guy in one night in bed than you do in months of
conversation. In the sack, they can't cheat.

—*Edith Piaf, soulful French singer*

It's never easy keeping your own husband happy. It's much easier to make someone else's husband happy.

—*Zsa Zsa Gabor, international actress and socialite*

I love the lines men use to get us into bed. "Please, I'll only put it in for a minute." What am I, a microwave?

—*Beverly Mickins, TV personality*

If someone had told me years ago that sharing a sense of humor was so vital to partnerships, I could have avoided a lot of sex!

—*Kate Beckinsale, brainy British actress*

Among men, sex sometimes results in intimacy; among women, intimacy sometimes results in sex.

—*Barbara Cartland, widely read British romance novelist*

A homely face and no figure have aided many women heavenward.

—Minna Antrim, turn-of-the-century wordsmith

If God had wanted women to be sex symbols he wouldn't have made Mary a virgin.

—Patti Harrison and Robin Tyler, dynamite comedy duo

However much men say sex is not on their mind all the time, it is most of the time.

—*Jackie Collins, romantic novelist*

Lovers should also have their days off.

—*Natalie Clifford Barney, turn-of-the-century Parisian hostess*

Any woman who thinks the way to a man's heart is through his stomach is aiming about ten inches too high.

—*Adrienne Gusoff, professional funny girl*

I have more sex appeal on the tip of my nose than many women in their entire bodies.

—*Audrey Hepburn, elfin icon*

I was like, "I want that one!"

I am not especially defined by my sex life, nor complete without it.

Personally, I like sex and I don't care what a man thinks of me as long as I get what I want from him—which is usually sex.

—*Valerie Perrine, film attraction*

If men knew what women laughed about, they would never sleep with us.

—*Erica Jong, American author of women's lit*

Everybody should practice safe sex. Cause nobody wants to be doing it and put an eye out.

—*Emmy Gay, "Fusion Art" entertainer*

Xi Shi

The beautiful Xi Shi was born in the Chinese state of Yue during the late sixth century B.C. She is known as one of the Four Beauties of ancient China, and like her three counterparts, she played a pivotal role in the political intrigues of her day. Xi Shi was described as being so lovely that the fish bowed their heads when she cleaned her garments in the river. When she was a young girl, King Gou Jian of Yue was defeated and taken prisoner by his rival, King Fu Chai of Wu. After Gou Jian's release, he concocted a plan to take revenge on his former captors. Xi Shi and another famed beauty were trained as subversive agents and sent to Fu Chai under the guise of tribute payment.

Fu Chai immediately fell under the spell of Xi Shi, neglecting his duties and lavishing the riches of his state upon his new consorts. At their request, he erected a luxurious palace in their honor and even arranged the murder of his most trusted advisor. His lust for Xi Shi was so great that it weakened the entire state of Wu; in

473 B.C., King Gou Jian crushed Fu Chai's army and regained his power in the region. Realizing that he had been destroyed by his blind love, Fu Chai committed suicide. The fate of Xi Shi herself is unknown. While some accounts hold that she was executed to save future rulers from her influence, others claim that she escaped to Tai Ho Lake and lived out her life in the wilderness.

Women complain about sex more than men. Their gripes fall into two major categories: 1) Not enough. 2) Too much.

—Ann Landers, advice guru

For women the best aphrodisiacs are words. The G-spot is in the ears. He who looks for it below there is wasting his time.

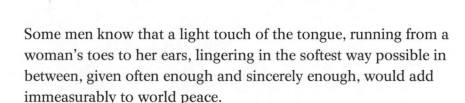

— *Isabel Allende, acclaimed Chilean American novelist*

Some men know that a light touch of the tongue, running from a woman's toes to her ears, lingering in the softest way possible in between, given often enough and sincerely enough, would add immeasurably to world peace.

— *Marianne Williamson, outspoken pacifist*

No one ever expects a great lay to pay all the bills.

—Jean Harlow, Hollywood star of the thirties

Sex: That pathetic shortcut suggested by nature the supreme joker as a remedy for our loneliness, that ephemeral communion which we persuade ourselves to be of the spirit when in fact it is only of the body—durable not even in memory!

—Vita Sackville-West, Bloomsbury author

Dr. Ruth says we should tell our lovers how to make love to us. My boyfriend goes nuts if I tell him how to drive!

—*Pam Stone, equestrienne comedian*

Ah, the sex thing. I'm glad that part of my life is over.

—*Greta Garbo, Swedish actress, at the age of sixty-nine*

Size Matters

When it comes to conversations about sex, there's one topic that almost always comes up eventually. Although women can never agree on it, the matter of size certainly plays a role in our sex lives—or at least our sex gossip.

According to darling Merle Oberon, Jimmy Cagney was "a REALLY big star!"

If Clark had one inch less, he'd be the "queen of Hollywood" instead of "the king."

—Carol Lombard, Clark Gable's third wife

He's no Tommy Lee, that's for sure.

—Unimpressed publicist who viewed copies of the paparazzi pix of Jude Law caught in the nude

In the United States of America, there are over 25,000 sex phone lines for men. You know how many there are for women? Just three. Apparently for women, if we want someone to talk dirty and nasty to us, we'll just go to work.

—*Felicia Michaels, hardworking comedian*

I need sex for a clear complexion, but I'd rather do it for love.

—*Joan Crawford, diva of classic Hollywood*

I haven't had sex in eight months. To be honest, I now prefer to go bowling.

—*Lil' Kim, notorious rapper*

If sex is such a natural phenomenon, how come there are so many books on how to?

—*Bette Midler, singer, actress, and comedian extraordinaire*

It is not sex that gives the pleasure, but the lover.

—*Marge Piercy, activist and author*

It doesn't make any difference what you do in the bedroom as long as you don't do it in the street and frighten the horses.

—*Mrs. Patrick Campbell, turn-of-the-century British stage actress*

I think the V line below a man's stomach is just really beautiful and sexy.

—*Kirstie Allie, formerly Fat Actress*

The argument between wives and whores is an old one; each one thinking that whatever she is, at least she is not the other.

—*Andrea Dworkin, radical feminist and author*

Marilyn Monroe

It's not as though Hollywood had never produced a sex symbol before, but no other actress (and arguably no other woman) has ever seized the American imagination like Marilyn Monroe. Lovelorn foster child, radiant sex goddess, presidential mistress, suicidal substance-abuser—as we all know, there are a million angles to Monroe's oft-told story. Her film career began with a surprisingly slow start. For several years, the future star could barely get past the casting couch. As she later admitted, she sometimes resorted to trading sexual favors for food. But her 1950 performance in *The Asphalt Jungle* resulted in an avalanche of fan mail, and breathless performances in several subsequent films made her into a genuine sex goddess.

Monroe, of course, had her own frustrations about being the source of so much prurient fascination. She yearned to do more in her movies than wiggle, pout, and demonstrate the erotic appeal of subway gratings. Then as now, "bombshell" was considered synonymous with "bimbo," and Monroe was mocked rather than applauded when she left Hollywood to study at the Strasberg's Actors' Studio in New York. Yet upon her return, she made *Bus Stop* (1956), considered by many to be her finest film. Her act of defiance also afforded her the opportunity to mingle with a more intellectual crowd; Albert Einstein was one of the sex symbol's own fantasy objects. While the Myth of Marilyn may be fueled by the erotic and even the seamy sides of Monroe's life, she was undeniably much more than a mere two-dimensional pinup.

I smoked a lot of dope. I made it with a lot of guys. I tried every way. I tried everything I could think of to act just as bad and outrageous as I could.

—*Elizabeth Ashley, Vargas girl and card-carrying wild woman*

So this is where I get laid!

—Silver-screen star Olive Thomas on her first meeting in
David O. Selznick's office, complete with casting couch

I like to drink and f**k.

—Louise Brooks, succinct silent film siren

Sexual love is the most stupendous fact of the universe, and the most magical
mystery our poor blind senses know.

—Amy Lowell, leading poet of the Imagist school

I've learned one hell of a lot about men in my lifetime. They're all right to take to bed, but you sure better never let them get a stranglehold on you.

—*Blaze Starr, sassy southern stripper*

Men are my hobby; if I ever got married, I'd have to give it up.

—*Mae West, legend of the silver screen*

Love Is a Pain

I love men, even though they're lying, cheating scumbags.

—*Gwyneth Paltrow, box-office phenomenon*

If a man lies to you, don't get mad, get even. I once dated a guy who waited three months into our relationship before he told me he was married. I said, "Hey, don't worry about it. I used to be a man."

—*Livia Squires, seismologist and comic*

I'm single. I'm skinny. I still can't find a man.

—*Sarah Ferguson, Duchess of York*

If love means never having to say you're sorry, then marriage means always having to say everything twice.

—*Estelle Getty, geriatric Golden Girl*

My biggest problem with dating is that I have no game. Some women can just bat their eyes and men come running. The men just keep popping up one after another. It's like they have a magical man-filled Pez dispenser.

—*Lori Giarnella, outspoken comedian*

The essence of romantic love is that wonderful beginning, after which sadness and impossibility may become the rule.

—*Anita Brookner, art historian and author*

You know, new lovers should really have a minimum isolation period of say, six months, so as not to nauseate absolutely everyone they meet.

—Kathy Lette, best-selling author

Women are cursed, and men are the proof.

—Rosanne Barr, actress and outspoken lady

We choose those we like; with those we love, we have no say in the matter.

—*Mignon McLaughlin, journalist and author*

If it has tires or testicles, you're going to have trouble with it.

—*Linda Furney, U.S. politician*

Saying that men talk about baseball in order to avoid talking about their feelings is the same as saying that women talk about their feelings in order to avoid talking about baseball.

—*Deborah Tannen, twentieth-century linguistics expert*

Women might be able to fake orgasms. But men can fake whole relationships.

—*Sharon Stone, always elegant and eloquent actress*

Deirdre of the Sorrows

Deirdre was a legendary beauty of ancient Ireland, whose love affair was fated
to bring war, sorrow, and death to both her lover and herself. Conor Mac Nessa,
the high king of Ulster, claimed her as his future bride before she was even born
after hearing a prophesy of her loveliness. To ensure that she was kept secret
from the eyes of other men, he sent her to be raised by a foster mother, the poetess
Levarcham. But Conor made a bad choice of keepers; Levarcham was determined
to save her charge from an empty marriage to the aged king. When Deirdre was
old enough, Levarcham sent her to meet the handsome youth Naoise, and the two
teenagers predictably fell in love. Although Naoise was reluctant to risk the king's
anger, Deirdre convinced him to run away with her, accompanied by his two
faithful brothers.

Despite several years of freedom, the couple was unable to escape the jealous wrath of Conor forever. After roaming through Ireland and Scotland and encountering various entanglements, Naoise and his brothers were tricked into returning to Ulster, where they were immediately slaughtered. Deirdre was inconsolable, and Conor eventually took revenge on her by attempting to pack her off to the warrior who had slain her love. But Deirdre tragically outsmarted him, leaping to her death during the journey from the palace. She was buried next to Naoise, and two intertwined pines grew from their graves, never to be parted.

> With lovers like men, who needs torturers?
>
> —*Susanne Kappeler, social sciences professor*

I'm like the Statue of Liberty. No one wants to pay for the upkeep, but everybody wants to say they've been there.

—*Priscilla Davis, Texas socialite*

Opposites attract—and then aggravate.

—*Joy Browne, radio psychologist*

Falling in love is no way of getting to know someone.

—Sheila Sullivan, psychologist

The advantage of love at first sight is that it delays a second sight.

—Natalie Clifford Barney, turn-of-the-century Parisian hostess

For me, on a scale of one to ten, romance comes about eighth, after chess but before politics and football.

—Alice Thomas Ellis, author of cookbooks and novels

All love shifts and changes. I don't know if you can be wholeheartedly in love all the time.

—Julie Andrews, wholesome singer and actress

Giving a man space is like giving a dog a computer: the chances are he will not use it wisely.

—*Bette-Jane Raphael, sharp satirist*

Sometimes I wonder if men and women really suit each other. Perhaps they should live next door and just visit now and then.

—*Katharine Hepburn, bold and beautiful screen legend*

The pain of love is the pain of being alive. It is a perpetual wound.

—*Maureen Duffy, British poet, playwright, and novelist*

The easiest kind of relationship for me is with ten thousand people. The hardest is with one.

—*Joan Baez, activist and folksinger*

It is better to be unfaithful than to be faithful without wanting to be.

—*Brigitte Bardot, quintessential sex kitten*

Women Love Movies About Love

Painful love often makes for some unpainful storylines. Here's a list of the weepiest chick flicks ever—grab a box of Kleenex, some chocolate, your best girlfriends, and turn the channel to "romance!"

The Way We Were

Featuring Barbra Streisand and Robert Redford as star-crossed soulmates— "Gorgeous goy guy" meets Jewish radical girl in this glossy romance.

Camille

Scandinavian siren Greta Garbo stars as a tragic courtesan turned heroine who has to sacrifice her own happiness in order to prove her love; a classic for all time.

The French Lieutenant's Woman

A movie from a book about a movie about a movie. Confused? Don't worry, just sit back and enjoy Meryl Streep at her most mesmerizing in her role as a woman abandoned by her French lieutenant lover, played by the stellar Jeremy Irons.

The Women

Starring Rosalind Russell, Norma Shearer, and Joan Crawford, the movie's tagline says it all: "The stars! The clothes! The cruelty! The catfights!" Husband-stealing vixens at each other's throats is also a fairly good description.

The English Patient

Mysterious count Ralph Fiennes has an affair with lovely Englishwoman Kristen Scott Thomas. This romance takes you to Northern Africa and Italy during World War II. Passion, danger, spies, lies, and redemption . . . what could be better?

Bull Durham

A romantic comedy love triangle featuring a majorly minor league baseball team, an aging groupie, a world-weary catcher, and a cocky rookie. Kevin Costner, Susan Sarandon, and Tim Robbins heat up on the screen and in real life, too!

The hardest-learned lesson: that people have only their kind of love to give, not our kind.

—*Mignon McLaughlin, journalist and author*

Part of the reason that men seem so much less loving than women is that men's behavior is measured with a feminine ruler.

—*Francesca M. Cancian, calculating wild woman*

Love is an exploding cigar we willingly smoke.

—*Lynda Barry, progressive cartoonist*

We don't believe in rheumatism and true love until after the first attack.

—*Marie von Ebner-Eschenbach, Austrian writer of psychological novels*

Romance is dead— it was acquired in a hostile takeover by Hallmark and Disney, homogenized, and sold off piece by piece.

—*Lisa Simpson, brainy cartoon sis*

Mumps, measles, and puppy love are terrible after twenty.

—*Mignon McLaughlin, journalist and author*

Before I met my husband, I'd never fallen in love. I'd stepped in it a few times.

—*Rita Rudner, sovereign of stand-up*

Love, love, love—all the wretched cant of it, masking egotism, lust, masochism, fantasy under a mythology of sentimental postures.

—*Germaine Greer, feminist academic, writer, and broadcaster*

Life is a quest and love a quarrel.

—*Edna St. Vincent Millay, legendary poet*

Have you ever been in love? Horrible, isn't it? It makes you so vulnerable. It opens your chest and it opens your heart and it means someone can get inside you and mess you up. You build up all these defenses. You build up this whole armor, for years, so nothing can hurt you, then one stupid person, no different from any other stupid person, wanders into your stupid life. . . ."

—*Rose Walker, amorous* Sandman *heroine*

There are men I could spend eternity with, but not this life.

—Kathleen Norris, prolific author

If only one could tell true love from false love as one can tell mushrooms from toadstools.

—Katherine Mansfield, respected short fiction author

It was the men I deceived the most that I loved the most.

—*Marguerite Duras, writer and director*

Romantic love, in pornography as in life, is the mythic celebration of female negation. For a woman, love is defined as her willingness to submit to her own annihilation. The proof of love is that she is willing to be destroyed by the one whom she loves, for his sake.

—*Andrea Dworkin, radical feminist and writer*

Well, love is insanity. The ancient Greeks knew that. It is the taking over of a rational and lucid mind by delusion and self-destruction. You lose yourself, you have no power over yourself, you can't even think straight.

—*Marilyn French, feminist novelist*

In a great romance, each person plays a part the other really likes.

—*Elizabeth Ashley, Vargas girl and card-carrying wild woman*

The fate of love is that it always seems too little or too much.

—*Amelia Barr, writer of semi-historical tales*

Love ceases to be a pleasure, when it ceases to be a secret.

—*Aphra Behn, Restoration-era dramatist*

Love matches are made by people who are content, for a month of honey, to condemn themselves to a life of vinegar.

—*Marguerite Gardiner, Irish popular novelist of the nineteenth century*

Love is not enough. It must be the foundation, the cornerstone—but not the complete structure. It is much too pliable, too yielding.

—*Bette Davis, blue-eyed screen siren*

Eleanor Roosevelt

Eleanor was born Anne Eleanor Roosevelt and came from colonial stock on both sides of her family. Though born to the privileged class, she reached out to all women, regardless of economic status, and they responded, knowing she was a kindred soul. She preferred to do good works at settlement houses among the working class rather than party at snooty salons. Eleanor also snuck in an engagement to her fifth cousin, political aspirant Franklin Delano Roosevelt. They quickly had six children, and the burgeoning clan found themselves in the District of Columbia while FDR served as assistant secretary of the navy. It was there that Eleanor discovered his affair with Lucy Mercer, her social secretary. She was devastated, but found an inner resolve to withstand the pain and became even more dedicated to social change.

When FDR was elected president, Eleanor was less than thrilled with her status as First Lady. But she took on the job and made it her own. She held a press conference in 1933, the first First Lady to do so, and regularly spoke with a corps of women reporters. While FDR had his fireside chats, Eleanor had "My Day," a newspaper column and radio show that she used as a pulpit to address many social justice issues. After her husband's death, she continued with her work, becoming a delegate to the United Nations and helping launch UNICEF. This humanitarian and strong woman is still one of the most cherished figures in history.

One would always want to think of oneself as being on the side of love, ready to recognize it and wish it well—but, when confronted with it in others, one so often resented it, questioned its true nature, secretly dismissed the particular instance as folly or promiscuity. Was it merely jealousy, or a reluctance to admit so noble and enviable a sentiment in anyone but oneself?

—*Shirley Hazzard, writer and novelist*

Women are like dogs really. They love like dogs, a little insistently. And they like to fetch and carry and come back wistfully after hard words, and learn rather easily to carry a basket."

—*Mary Roberts Rinehart, author of murder mysteries*

Smart women love smart men more than smart men love smart women.

—*Natalie Portman, brainy actress*

I have never wanted to be one of those girls in love with boys who would not have me. Unrequited love—plain desperate aboveboard boy-chasing—turned you into a salesperson, and what you were selling was something he didn't want, could not use, would never miss. Unrequited love was deciding to be useless, and I could never abide uselessness.

—Elizabeth McCraken, short fiction writer

I have yet to hear a man ask for advice on how to combine marriage and a career.

—Gloria Steinem, founder of Ms. *magazine*

Great passions, my dear, don't exist: they're liars' fantasies.
What do exist are little loves that may last for a short or a longer
while.

—*Anna Magnani, tempestuous actress*

We live in a terrible world. A man kisses your hand and it's screamed out from
all the headlines. He can't even tell you he loves you without the whole world
knowing about it.

—*Grace Kelly, a princess with a past*

Marriage—it is like signing your life away.

—Julie Christie, self-aware actress and spinster

He's the equivalent of a dirt sandwich.

—Sharon Stone, always elegant and eloquent actress, describing her ex

He thought more of making love to the camera than to me.

—Jean Acker, who divorced Rudolph Valneit after a six-hour marriage

Lovers are at all times insufferable; but when the holy laws of matrimony give them the right to be so amazingly fond and affectionate, it makes one sick.

—Lady Caroline Lamb, notorious aristocrat

Any woman can marry if she sets her standards low enough.

—Deidre Marion Charlot, Myra Hayward Marion's mother

Love Lost

When two people decide to get a divorce, it isn't a sign that they "don't understand" one another, but a sign that they have, at last, begun to.

—*Helen Rowland, witty journalist*

I've had diseases that lasted longer than my marriages.

—*Nell Carter, beloved singer and actress*

Love lasts about seven years. That's how long it takes for the cells of the body to totally replace themselves.

—*Francoise Sagan, quintessential French writer*

It's afterward you realize that the feeling of happiness you had with a man didn't necessarily prove that you loved him.

—*Marguerite Duras, French filmmaker*

We were incompatible in a lot of ways. Like for example, I was a night person, and he didn't like me.

—*Wendy Liebman, winner of the American Comedy Award*

My attitude toward men who mess around is simple: If you find 'em, kill 'em.

—*Loretta Lynn, vengeful country songstress*

Love never dies of starvation, but often of indigestion.

—*Ninon de Lenclos, seventeenth-century French courtesan*

There were three of us in the marriage, so it was a bit crowded.

—*Diana, Princess of Wales*

I still miss my ex-husband, but my aim is improving.

—Debbie Marsh, comical pistol owner

I have always found husbands much more satisfying after marriage than during.

—Peggy Guggenheim, patron of the arts

Don't put an absurdly high value on him. Think of the millions of other girls doing without him, yet able to bear it!

—Orfea Sybil, unsung wit

I'm not upset about my divorce, I am only upset I'm not a widow.

—Unknown wild woman

I should be groaning over the sins I have committed, but I can only sigh for what I have lost.

—*Heloise, medieval nun and former lover of the famed scholar Abelard*

I still miss those I loved who are no longer with me but I find I am grateful for having loved them. The gratitude has finally conquered the loss.

—*Rita Mae Brown, activist author*

Heloise

Famed abbess Heloise lived during the twelfth century, attaining high standing as both a religious figure and a scholar during a time when most women were barred from the public sphere. Although she ended her days consecrated to the Catholic Church, Heloise's youth was marked with romantic intrigue and loss. Though not much is known of her background, she was raised by her uncle, Fulbert, a Parisian cleric. Recognizing her extreme intelligence, Fulbert encouraged Heloise's education, and she became locally famous for her learning in the areas of philosophy and language. When Heloise was eighteen, her continued schooling was entrusted to Peter Abelard, one of the most respected philosophers of the day. The two became lovers, but their happiness was short-lived.

When Fulbert discovered the extent of Abelard's involvement with his niece, the enraged cleric arranged for thugs to attack and castrate the scholar. Heloise, pregnant with Abelard's son, was spirited off to a convent, where she was pressed to take vows by both her lover and uncle. After the birth of her child, she took the veil, going on to attain the respect and acclaim of her contemporaries. Heloise eventually initiated a written correspondence with Abelard, who had himself taken vows with the Church. The pair sustained a primarily theological and philosophical discourse, but the surviving letters attest to the fact that Heloise, at least, never completely gave up her love for her former tutor.

In Hollywood, an equitable divorce settlement means each party getting fifty percent of the publicity.

—Lauren Bacall, husky and sultry icon

To live in this world you must be able to do three things: to love what is mortal; to hold it against your bones knowing your own life depends on it; and, when the time comes to let it go, to let it go."

—Mary Oliver, nature-loving poet

Moments of kindness and reconciliation are worth having, even if the parting has to come sooner or later.

—*Alice Munro, acclaimed writer of short fiction*

Have some good revenge fantasies. Hate his guts if that makes you feel better!

—*Marni Kamen,* Breakup Repair *gal*

Deep down, we knew there wasn't a forever plan.

—*Naomi Watts, King Kong's true love, on her breakup with Heath Ledger*

I was never one to patiently pick up broken fragments and glue them together again and tell myself that the mended whole was as good as new. What is broken is broken—and I'd rather remember it as it was at its best than mend it and see the broken places as long as I lived.

—*Margaret Mitchell, quintessential southern wild woman*

Real loss only occurs when you lose something that you love more than yourself.

—*Unknown wild woman*

It's a long road when you face the world alone, when no one reaches out a hand for you to hold. You can find love if you search within your soul, and the emptiness you felt will disappear.

—*Mariah Carey, resilient chart-topper*

When It's Time to Get Lost

Sure, it hurts, but sometimes you just gotta cut somebody loose. Trust us, you'll feel better once it's done. Here are a few warning signs, courtesy of breakup and healing experts Marni Kamins and Janice MacLeod, authors of *The Breakup Repair Kit*.

- When you're making love, you'd rather be reading a magazine.
- Your eyes glaze over when he talks.
- He tells you things you don't agree with and you choose to ignore them.
- You know in your heart that if he wasn't paying for the meal, you'd rather be eating it with someone else.

- He's a dick to his mom—definitely a stop sign. How he treats his mother is how he will eventually treat you.

- You find yourself wondering if he gets skidmarks in his underwear.

And for those of you already dealing with a lost love, hang in there! Give yourself lots of TLC, and soon you'll be getting it from someone else again.

I wanted a perfect ending. Now I've learned, the hard way, that some poems don't rhyme, and some stories don't have a clear beginning, middle, and end. Life is about not knowing, having to change, taking the moment and making the best of it, without knowing what's going to happen next.

—*Gilda Radner, original* SNL *funny girl*

I could do without many things with no hardship—you are not one of them.

—*Ashleigh Brilliant, author and cartoonist*

Love never dies a natural death. It dies because we don't know how to replenish its source. It dies of blindness and errors and betrayals. It dies of illness and wounds; it dies of weariness, of withering, of tarnishing.

—*Anaïs Nin, legendary writer and diarist*

However often marriage is dissolved, it remains indissoluble. Real divorce, the divorce of heart and nerve and fiber, does not exist, since there is no divorce from memory.

—*Virgilia Peterson, author and TV personality*

A divorce is like an amputation, you survive, but there's less of you.

—*Margaret Atwood, famed feminist author*

After all my erstwhile dear,
my no longer cherished;
Need we say it was not love,
just because it perished?

—*Edna St. Vincent Millay, legendary poet*

Always remember: this, too, shall pass.

—*Charlotte Chow, self-proclaimed breakup guru*

If you love someone, let them go. If they return to you, it was meant to be. If they don't, their love was never yours to begin with.

—*Unknown wild woman*

When once estrangement has arisen between those who truly love each other, everything seems to widen the breach.

—*Mary Elizabeth Braddon, British novelist, playwright, and editor*

A bizarre sensation pervades a relationship of pretense. No truth seems true. A simple morning's greeting and response appear loaded with innuendo and fraught with implications. Each nicety becomes more sterile and each withdrawal more permanent.

—*Maya Angelou, soulful American writer*

Diana, Princess of Wales

One of the most iconic figures of our time, Diana, Princess of Wales, lived her life—and her tumultuous marriage—under the constant gaze of the media eye. Her engagement and marriage to Prince Charles in 1981 was regarded by many as an idyllic fairy tale romance, complete with wedding ring and royal crown. However, when the public fantasy became an equally public separation, Diana's celebrity took on a new dimension. Until her tragic death in a 1997 car crash, believed to be caused at least in part by a group of pursuing paparazzi, she remained both the most beloved and the most gossiped about woman in the world. Controversy surrounding the details of her life and death continues today.

But Diana's legacy was equally defined by her respected and influential charity work, most notably in the areas of AIDS awareness and anti-landmine activism. Rather than being limited by the ups and downs of her very public private affairs,

Diana channeled her fame to support causes she was passionate about. She is credited with helping break down the social stigma of the AIDS epidemic and with encouraging international support for the Ottawa Treaty, which bans the use of anti-personnel landmines. As a champion of positive change and an example of perseverance in the face of personal loss and pain, Diana remains a true role model in the eyes of many women.

Two separate, distinct personalities, not separate at all, but inextricably bound, soul and body and mind, to each other, how did we get so far apart so fast?

—*Judith Guest, novelist and screenwriter*

Falling out of love is chiefly a matter of forgetting how charming someone is.

—*Iris Murdoch, British author*

How lucky I am to have known someone so hard to say good-bye to.

—*Unknown wild woman*

If we deny love that is given to us, if we refuse to give love because we fear the pain of loss, then our lives will be empty, our loss greater.

—*Margaret Weis and Tracy Hickman, fantastical female authors*

Only when you are lost can love find itself in you without losing its way.

—*Helene Cixous , French feminist writer*

A broken heart is what makes life so wonderful—five years later.

—*Phyllis Battelle, brainy reporter*

Some people think it's holding on that makes one strong; sometimes it's letting go.

—*Sylvia Robinson, singer, musician, and producer*

Parrots, tortoises, and redwoods live a longer life than men do; men a longer life than dogs do; dogs a longer life than love does.

—*Edna St. Vincent Millay, legendary poet*

If love means that one person absorbs the other, then no real relationship exists any more. Love evaporates; there is nothing left to love. The integrity of self is gone.

—*Ann Oakley, feminist Brit*

We who were loved will never unlive that crippling fever.
—*Adrienne Rich, renowned radical poet and feminist*

Love is the direct opposite of hate. By definition it's something you can't feel for more than a few minutes at a time, so what's all this bullshit about loving somebody for the rest of your life?

—*Judith Rossner, novelist of the sexual liberation movement*

Are Men Really
Necessary ?

For a long time I thought I wanted to be a nun. Then I realized that what I really wanted to be was a lesbian.

—Mabel Maney, creator of Nancy Clue and the Hardly Boys

Free love? As if love is anything but free! Man has bought brains, but all the millions in the world have failed to buy love. Man has subdued bodies, but all the power on earth has been unable to subdue love. Man has conquered whole nations, but all his armies could not conquer love. Man has chained and fettered the spirit, but he has been utterly helpless before love. High on a throne, with all the splendor and pomp his gold can command, man is yet poor and desolate, if love passes him by. And if it stays, the poorest hovel is radiant with warmth, with life and color. Thus love has the magic power to make of a beggar a king. Yes, love is free; it can dwell in no other atmosphere.

—Emma Goldman, anarcha-feminist groundbreaker

What do you mean, you "don't believe in homosexuality"? It's not like the Easter Bunny, your belief isn't necessary.

—*Lea Delaria, proud comic and musician*

I believed that the best way to get to know a woman was to go to bed with her . . . so pretty much everywhere I've lived I've had a real bad reputation. But it has gotten me a lot of interesting dates.

—*Dorothy Allison, best-selling bad girl*

I've had long-term sexual relationships with both men and women. If that classifies me as bisexual, then I'm bisexual.

—Sandra Bernhard, show biz's lippy lady

The infantile needs of adult men for women have been sentimentalized and romanticized long enough as "love"; it is time to recognize them as arrested development.

—Adrienne Rich, renowned radical poet and feminist

If love is the answer, could you rephrase the question?

—Lily Tomlin, talented lesbian actress

For her, and her alone, I could have been a lesbian.

—Joan Crawford gabbing about Greta Garbo

My lesbianism is an act of Christian charity. All those women out there praying for a man, and I'm giving them my share.

—*Rita Mae Brown, activist author*

In itself, homosexuality is as limiting as heterosexuality: the ideal should be to be capable of loving a woman or a man; either, a human being, without feeling fear, restraint, or obligation.

—*Simone de Beauvoir, unconventional philosopher*

Sappho

Lyric poet Sappho is widely regarded as the greatest writer of ancient times. She came to be known as the "tenth muse." While scholars can't agree whether Homer even existed, Sappho's work was recorded and preserved by other writers. Although she is believed to have been married and had one daughter, much of her work is written to other women, exalting them for their beauty and often achieving a poetic frenzy of desire. She also makes references to the political arena of the ancient world she inhabited.

An unfortunate destruction of a volume of all her work—nine books of lyric poetry and one of elegiac verse—occurred in the early Middle Ages, engendering a search for her writing that continues even now. The Catholic Church deemed her poetry to be obscene and burned the only volume containing her complete body of work, thus erasing what could only be some of the finest poetry in all of history. Known for its powerful phrasing and intensity of feeling, erotic and otherwise,

Sappho's poetry is immediately striking and accessible to the reader. Upon reading Sappho, you feel that you know her, both her ecstatic highs and her painful longings. Her writing remains some of the most beautiful expressions of lesbian passion, and she is regarded stylistically to be the first modern poet.

My mom blames California for me being a lesbian. "Everything was fine until you moved out there." "That's right, Mom, we have mandatory lesbianism in West Hollywood. The Gay Patrol busted me, and I was given seven business days to add a significant amount of flannel to my wardrobe."

—*Coley Sohn, humorous lesbian gal*

We love men. We just don't want to see them naked.

—*Two Nice Girls, queer country rockers*

When you're in love you never really know whether your elation comes from the qualities of the one you love, or if it attributes them to her; whether the light which surrounds her like a halo comes from you, from her, or from the meeting of your sparks.

—*Natalie Clifford Barney, turn-of-the-century Parisian hostess*

Every woman I have ever loved has left her print upon me, where I loved some invaluable piece of myself apart from me—so different that I had to stretch and grow in order to recognize her. And in that growing, we came to separation, that place where work begins.

—*Audre Lorde, award-winning poet*

I was raised around heterosexuals . . . that's where us gay people come from.

—*Ellen DeGeneres, queen of queer comedy*

I can play a heterosexual. I know how they walk. I know how they talk. You don't have to be one to play one.

—*Lily Tomlin, talented lesbian actress*

Are there many things in this cool-hearted world so utterly exquisite as the pure love of one woman for another?

—*Mary MacLane, wild writer of the early 1900s*

Hick darling . . . I couldn't say "je t'aime et je t'adore" as I longed to do, but always remember I am saying it, that I go to sleep thinking of you.

—*Eleanor Roosevelt, in a letter to Lorena Hickok*

Power Couples

Lesbians, bisexuals, and nonstraight women of all types have been around forever, from the literary world to the high seas. Just take a look at this extremely abbreviated list of famous devoted ladies!

Willa Cather, author, and Edith Lewis

Gertrude Stein, author and poet, and Alice B. Toklas, author

Katharine Lee Bates, poet and Wellesley College professor, and Katharine Coman, Wellesley College dean (Bates wrote the poem "America the Beautiful")

Angelina Weld Grimké, author and famed abolitionist, and Mamie Burrill

Sara Teasdale, poet, and Margaret Conklin

Susan Sontag, author and critic, and Annie Liebovitz, photographer

Lady Eleanor Butler and Sarah Ponsonby, eighteenth-century Brits (*The General Evening Post* referred to them as the "Ladies of Llangeollen" in 1790)

Anne Cormac Bonny and Mary Read, pirates (These two outlaws were brought to trial in 1720.)

I'm a "trisexual." I'll try anything once.
—*Samantha (a.k.a. Kim Catrall), on* Sex and the City

What is a Lesbian? A Lesbian is a woman who loves women, who counts on women for her emotional support, who looks to women for her growth, who finds her identity in her womanhood. A Lesbian is a woman who, more and more willingly, and with more and more pride, knows and shows her own strength, makes her own definitions for herself, and dares to defy society's most sacred taboo—"Thou shalt not live without men and like it."

—*Ginny Berson and Robin Brooks, gutsy wild women*

We women are the best thing going—we are warm, passionate, we cry and we live! Let's celebrate!

—*Margaret Sloan-Hunter, feminist and civil rights advocate*

I think [that] in love, there's not sex, there's not segregation, there's not anything, there's just LOVE, and that's what I feel. . . . I don't feel like I'm coming out. I've never been in a closet. I've never had anything to hide. I've lived my life in truth always. This was just a natural progression toward getting more love in my life.

—*Anne Heche, actress and Ellen deGeneres's former paramour*

If love does not know how to give and take without restrictions, it is not love, but a transaction that never fails to lay stress on a plus and a minus.

—*Emma Goldman, anarcha-feminist groundbreaker*

I became a lesbian because of women, because women are beautiful, strong, and compassionate.

—*Rita Mae Brown, activist author*

I think God is a callous bitch not making me a lesbian. I'm deeply disappointed by my sexual interest in men.

—*Diamanda Galas, jealous musician*

Audre Lorde

A black lesbian poet who never hid her truth, Audre Lorde started writing poetry seriously in grade school. Her parents were West Indian immigrants who escaped to New York City from Grenada in 1924, just in time for the Great Depression. Dazzlingly bright, Audre read voraciously. After a stint at the University of Mexico, where the atmosphere of racial tolerance opened her eyes to racism in the United States, she began attending Hunter College and earned a degree in library science from Columbia. She married and had two children while working for several New York libraries. After her divorce, she again moved toward her true passion—creative writing. She went on to teach writing at many prestigious schools throughout America, where her reputation as an extraordinarily gifted poet grew.

In 1982, Lorde published *Ami: a New Spelling of My Name*, a work she considered the literary outing of her lesbianism. A staunch feminist and political activist, she decried the sexism and hypocrisy of her times in poems such as "Cables to Rage" and "The Black Unicorn." Though she began in coffeehouses and humble church basements, she was soon filling theatres and garnering national honors, including the American Book Award. She also became New York's poet laureate shortly before losing her life to breast cancer in 1992. Audre Lorde is a true poet's poet, an inspiration to both writers and women everywhere.

But I always have and still do consider myself queer. To me, being queer isn't who you're sleeping with; it's just an idea that sexuality isn't gender-based, that it's love-based."

—*Ani DiFranco, gutsy folksinger, in response to criticism for loving a male*

I wear a T-shirt that says "The family tree stops here."

—*Suzanne Westenhoefer, comic and proud homosexual*

Pronouns make it hard to keep our sexual orientation a secret when our coworkers ask us about our weekend. "I had a great time with . . . them." Great! Now they don't think you're queer—just a big slut!

—*Judy Carter, lesbian comedienne*

My father warned me about men and booze, but he never mentioned a word about women and cocaine.

—*Tallulah Bankhead, adventurous gal and PR pioneer*

Anyone who's being honest has to admit that what we've got is exponentially more attractive than what they've got.

—*Becky K. Ambler, tough and gorgeous wild woman*

Strong Women, Strong Love

My honour was not yielded, but conquered merely.

—Cleopatra, quintessential temptress queen

No husband of mine will say, "I could have been a drummer, but I had to think about the wife and kids. You know how it is." Nobody supports me at the expense of his own adventure.

—Maxine Hong Kingston, Asian American author and sage

Ted needs someone to be there 100 percent of the time. He thinks that's love. It's not love—it's babysitting.

—*Jane Fonda, activist actress*

I don't want to say that I want a man to like me for my mind, because that's going to sound like I think I'm Albert Einstein. But I would like someone who doesn't accuse me of making up words like "segue."

—*Mariah Carey, resilient chart-topper*

Better an old man's darling than a young man's slave.

> —*Alberta Martin, the "Oldest Living Confederate Widow,"*
> *who married a man sixty years her senior*

Basically, I've dodged that marriage bullet. . . . I like the jewelry part of getting married, but I can buy my own damn things, too.

> — *Queen Latifah, rap royalty*

Men are always ready to respect anything that bores them.

—Marilyn Monroe, ultimate blond bombshell

It is no longer obligatory upon a woman to give herself to one man to save herself from being torn to pieces by the rest.

—Jane Cunningham Croly, founder of the nineteenth-century woman's club movement

The fantasy that we are overwhelmed by Rhett Butler should be traded in for one in which we seize state power and reeducate him.

—Sandra Lee Bartky, philosophy professor

Scratch most feminists and underneath there is a woman who longs to be a sex object. The difference is that is not all she wants to be.

—Betty Rollin, television correspondent and breast cancer expert

No pressure, no diamonds.

—*Mary Case, indie film screenwriter*

Trouble is part of your life—if you don't share it, you don't give the person who loves you a chance to love you enough.

—*Dinah Shore, singer, actress, and talk show host*

Penthesilea

The daughter of Orithia, Penthesilea was the ruler of Amazonia, the Bronze Age nation in an area of the Black Sea. Considered the greatest Amazon of all times, she was a fierce warrior; her name means "compelling men to mourn." Although the nation of Amazonia itself was peaceful and self-sufficient, its women warriors were regarded as the most highly skilled soldiers in the world. Even the Argonauts, the piratical adventurers of myth, dropped their plans to invade after observing the strength of Amazonia's army.

Penthesilea's zeal for battle was fueled by her grief and rage after the death of her sister. At the request of Queen Hecuba, she liberated the city of Troy, which had been under siege by the Greeks for years. Many scholars believe that Homer adapted his famous story of the Trojan War from an account by the Egyptian poetess Phantasia, rewriting it to cater to the patriarchal tastes of his Greek audience. The consensus among herstorians is that Penthesilea crossed swords with Achilles during the war and that the great Greek warrior fell deeply in love with her. Differing versions of the legend depict her as both the victor and the slain in the duel, but all agree she proved to be the only soldier Achilles ever encountered who was his equal.

We can do no great things; only small things with great love.
—*Mother Teresa, legendary selfless philanthropist*

It is really asking too much of a woman to expect her to bring up her husband and her children too.

—*Lillian Bell, overextended wild woman*

Him that I love, I wish to be free even from me.

—*Anne Morrow Lindbergh, aviatrix and author*

You don't have to be anti-man to be pro-woman.

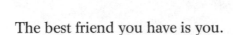

—*Jane Galvin Lewis, founder of the National Black Feminist Organization*

The best friend you have is you.

—*Carol Wiseman, author of comforting advice*

Friendship with oneself is all important because without it one cannot be friends with anybody else in the world.

—*Eleanor Roosevelt, self-assured First Lady*

I have an everyday religion that works for me. Love yourself first, and everything else falls into line.

—*Lucille Ball, ultimate wild redhead*

I love people. I love my family, my children . . . but inside myself is a place where I live all alone, and that's where you renew your springs that never dry up.

—*Pearl S. Buck, Nobel Prize-winning author*

People, even more than things, have to be restored, renewed, revived, reclaimed, and redeemed; never throw out anyone.

—*Audrey Hepburn, elfin icon*

No person is your friend who demands your silence, or denies your right to grow.

—Alice Walker, award-winning African American author

The love of our neighbor in all its fullness simply means being able to say, "What are you going through?"

—Simone Weil, French philosopher and mystic

I'd kiss a frog even if there was no promise of a Prince Charming popping out of it. I love frogs.

—*Cameron Diaz, actress and pop-culture fixture*

I think the reason we're so crazy sexually in America is that all our responses are acting. We don't know how to feel. We know how it looked in the movies.

—*Jill Robinson, trend tracker*

Friends: Our *Other* Significant Others

Any wild woman knows that her lovers aren't the only people in her life who deserve love and devotion. Here's to the women who stand by us when we really need it—our friends.

A friend is someone who reaches for your hand but touches your heart.
—*Kathleen Grove, inspiring wild woman*

Best friends are better than boyfriends!
—*Mavis Jukes, award-winning children's author*

The most beautiful discovery that true friends can make is that you can grow separately without growing apart.
—*Elizabeth Foley, healer and teacher*

Money might make you wealthy, but friends make you rich!

—*Margery Penney, secure wild woman*

A friend is someone who knows all about you and loves you anyway!

—*Leslie Rossman, wise woman and friend*

You don't make friends, you earn them!

—*Deena Patel Wine, wild sage*

I can trust my friends. These people force me to examine and encourage me to grow.

—*Cher, persevering pop icon*

A friend is someone who knows the song in your heart, and gives it back to you when you have forgotten the words.

—*Donna Roberts, musical wild woman*

If you judge people, you have no time to love them.

—Mother Teresa, legendary selfless philanthropist

A real friend is one who walks in when the rest of the world walks out.

—Beth Bachtold, thoughtful writer

The sharing of joy, whether physical, emotional, psychic, or intellectual, forms a bridge between the sharers which can be the basis for understanding much of what is not shared between them, and lessens the threat of their difference.

—Audre Lorde, award-winning poet

I always felt that the great high privilege, relief, and comfort of friendship was that one had to explain nothing.

—Katherine Mansfield, respected short fiction author

We all need friends with whom we can speak of our deepest concerns, and who do not fear to speak the truth in love to us.

—*Margret Guenther, truthful wild woman*

Though friendship is not quick to burn, it is explosive stuff.

—*May Sarton, poet and novelist*

When one is out of touch with oneself, one cannot touch others.

—*Anne Morrow Lindbergh, aviatrix and author*

It seems to me that trying to live without friends is like milking a bear to get cream for your morning coffee. It is a whole lot of trouble, and then not worth much after you get it.

—*Zora Neale Hurston, barrier-breaking novelist*

Friendship is the finest balm for the pangs of despised love.

—*Jane Austen, celebrated wit and novelist*

Women of my generation, unlike generations before us, we have been with several men—or in some cases, many men. I raise the question, why?

—*Joni Mitchell, groundbreaking folksinger*

Self-help books are making life downright unsafe. Women desperate to catch a man practice all the ploys recommended by these authors. Bump into him, trip over him, knock him down, spill something on him, scald him, but meet him.

— *Florence King, writer and self-styled misanthrope*

Nothing melts a woman's heart like gold.
> —*Susannah Centlivre, prolific playwright of the eighteenth century*

I wanted to make it really special on Valentine's Day, so I tied my boyfriend up. And for three solid hours I watched whatever I wanted to on TV.
> —*Tracy Smith, comedian extraordinaire*

The most important thing in a relationship between a man and a woman is that one of them must be good at taking orders.

—Linda Festa, widely quoted wit

Women have one great advantage over men. It is commonly thought that if they marry they have done enough and need career no further. If a man marries, on the other hand, public opinion is all against him if he takes this view.

—Rose Macaulay, named Dame of the British Empire for her prose

These are very confusing times. For the first time in history a woman is expected to combine intelligence with a sharp hairdo, a raised consciousness with high heels, and an open, nonsexist relationship with a tan guy who has a great bod.

—*Lynda Barry, progressive cartoonist*

The ultimate test of a relationship is to disagree but to hold hands.

—*Alexandra Penney, women's magazine writer and editor*

Men who consistently leave the toilet seat up secretly want women to get up to go to the bathroom in the middle of the night and fall in.

—Rita Rudner, sovereign of stand-up

Maybe I've been married a few too many times. I love a good party, but I have recently realized that I can actually just throw a party and not get married.

—Whoopi Goldberg, First Lady of comedy

Behind every successful man is a surprised woman.

—*Maryon Pearson, Canadian wit*

If you want to say it with flowers, a single rose says: "I'm cheap!"

—*Delta Burke, classic southern belle*

In real love you want the other person's good. In romantic love you want the other person.

—*Margaret Anderson, founder and editor of* The Little Review

I love humanity but I hate people.

Edna St Vincent Millay, legendary poet

No one can understand love who has not experienced infatuation. And no one can understand infatuation, no matter how many times he has experienced it.

—Mignon McLaughlin, journalist and author

Everyone of us needs to show how much we care for each other and, in the process, care for ourselves.

—Diana, Princess of Wales

Everyone admits that love is wonderful and necessary, yet no one agrees on just what it is.

—*Diane Ackerman, poet and nonfiction writer*

You can't put a price tag on love, but you can on all its accessories.

—*Melanie Clark, fashion-conscious wild woman*

Love is a fire. But whether it is going to warm your hearth or burn down your house, you can never tell.

—*Joan Crawford, diva of classic Hollywood*

If one doesn't respect oneself one can have neither love nor respect for others.

—*Ayn Rand, author and philosopher*

The ultimate lesson all of us have to learn is unconditional love, which includes not only others but ourselves as well.

—Elizabeth Kubler-Ross, Swiss-born psychiatrist and writer

A woman's love is a man's privilege, not his right.

—Unknown wild woman

Laugh and the world laughs with you. Cry and you cry with your girlfriends.

—*Laurie Kuslansky, supportive wit*

Simone de Beauvoir

Existentialist writer Simone de Beauvoir was the leader of the feminist movement in France and the dedicated (though unconventional) partner of Jean-Paul Sartre. Her book *The Second Sex* immediately took a place in the feminist canon upon its publication in 1949 and established Beauvoir's reputation as a leading thinker. She described traditional female roles as those of "relative beings" dependent on context, urging women to go after careers and achieve fulfillment through meaningful endeavors beyond what had previously been allowed. She met Sartre in her early twenties in a salon study group at famed Paris university the Sorbonne. They recognized each other as soul mates and remained together for fifty-one years. Although they had difficulty protecting their privacy as their international prestige heightened, they maintained a strong bond without limiting their capacity for enriching experience.

Beauvoir's first published works were fictional, including 1943's *She Came to Stay*, a novelized account of the life of Sartre's protégée Olga Kosakiewicz. Next, she tackled the male point of view in the epic novel treatment of death *All Men Are Mortal*. After the success of her feminist classic, Beauvoir returned to fiction with *The Mandarins*, which won the illustrious Goncourt Prize. She continued to write and publish until the end of her life, creating a weighty body of work. She died in 1986, outliving Sartre and leaving a legacy of contributions to gender and identity issues as well as philosophy and literature.

Start living now. Stop saving the good china for that special occasion. Stop withholding your love until that special person materializes. Every day you are alive is a special occasion. Every minute, every breath, is a gift from God.

—*Mary Manin, spiritual sage*

Just don't give up trying to do what you really want to do. Where there is love and inspiration, I don't think you can go wrong.

—*Ella Fitzgerald, passionate songstress*

I don't know about you, but I am glad my sweetheart is not a mind-reader.

—*Mary Jane Ryan, randomly kind actor*

Love is what we were born with. Fear is what we learned here.

—*Marianne Williamson, outspoken pacifist*

Women measure their achievements not in the wealth they have gathered but in the love they have gathered around them.

—*Linda Macfarlane, truly successful wild woman*

Not in strength are we inferior to men; the same our eyes, our limbs the same; one common light we see, one air we breathe; nor different is the food we eat. What then denied to us hath heaven on man bestowed?

—*Penthesilea, mythical Amazon queen*

TO OUR READERS

Conari Press, an imprint of Red Wheel/Weiser, publishes books on topics ranging from spirituality, personal growth, and relationships to women's issues, parenting, and social issues. Our mission is to publish high-quality books that will make a difference in people's lives—how we feel about ourselves and how we relate to one another. We value integrity, compassion, and receptivity, both in the books we publish and in the way we do business.

Our readers are our most important resource, and we value your input, suggestions, and ideas about what you would like to see published. Please feel free to contact us, to request our latest book catalog, or to be added to our mailing list.

Conari Press

An imprint of Red Wheel/Weiser, LLC

500 Third Street, Suite 230

San Francisco, CA 94107

www.redwheelweiser.com